Disappeared

A play

Phyllis Nagy

Samuel French — London
New York - Toronto - Hollywood

Please see page iv for further copyright information

DISAPPEARED

First produced by the Leicester Haymarket and Midnight
Theatre Company, in association with Chapman Duncan
Associates, at the Haymarket Studio, Leicester, on 2nd
February 1995 with the following cast:

Sarah Casey	Alexandra Gilbreath
Elston Rupp	Kerry Shale
Jack Fallon	Thomas Craig
Ellen Casey	Anna Keaveney
Ted Mitchell	Richard Bremmer
Natalie	Melee Hutton
Timothy Creighton	Steven Elder
Anthony	Eric Loren

Directed by Phyllis Nagy
Designed by Tim Shortall
Lighting by Johanna Town

Subsequently presented in London at the Royal Court
Theatre. First performed in the Theatre Upstairs on 27th
June 1995, produced by Leicester Haymarket and
Chapman Duncan Associates, with the following cast:

Sarah Casey	Alexandra Gilbreath
Elston Rupp	Kerry Shale
Jack Fallon	Thomas Craig
Ellen Casey	Anna Keaveney
Ted Mitchell	Andrew Woodall
Natalie	Melee Hutton
Timothy Creighton	Steven Elder
Anthony	Eric Loren

Directed by Phyllis Nagy
Designed by Tim Shortall
Lighting by Johanna Town

CHARACTERS

Elston Rupp
A small, nondescript man of indeterminate age. Impeccably groomed in a very odd way.

Sarah Casey
A 25-year-old travel agent who's never been anywhere.

Jack Fallon
A 26-year-old bartender who believes everything he reads in the tabloids.

Ellen Casey
Sarah's disappointed mother.

Ted Mitchell
A New York City homicide detective whose physical appearance and dry demeanour suggest he's something other than what he is.

Anthony
Sarah's boyfriend. An Italian-American hairdresser with a magnificent body and little else. Sweet and good-natured, he's the kind of man who doesn't understand hairdresser jokes.

Natalie
Elston's employer. She owns a thrift shop she doesn't want. She wears only brand new clothes, and never wears anything more than once.

Timothy Creighton
An entertainment attorney in his forties. Painfully shy, for a lawyer.

SYNOPSIS OF SCENES

The action takes place in New York City

Time — one Sunday evening, and at various times preceding and following that evening

For Pat, with love and thanks

AUTHOR'S NOTES

The Set

The setting should represent a barren landscape with touches of the other-worldly. It should appear as if everything here, while maintaining certain aspects of naturalism, appears from nowhere.

The Text

The use of capitals in certain passages does not necessarily or exclusively indicate a rise in speaking volume. However, the capitalization always suggests a shift in intensity or emphasis. Similarly, the use of "beats" does not suggest the use of pauses. Rather, the beats indicate shifts in thought, sometimes quite abrupt shifts. The punctuation often does not conform to standard punctuation as sentences are sometimes broken where one might not expect them to be broken, and often what might naturally be written as a question is written as a statement. Strict attention should therefore be paid to the punctuation pattern as it does create the text's rhythm. Black-outs should not be used at all as the action from scene to scene should proceed with fluidity. The music selected for the play is not random. It relates very specifically to the text; therefore, no substitutions should be made.

ACT I

SCENE 1

O'Malley's saloon, a seedy, run-down bar, Hell's Kitchen, New York City

As the House Lights dim there is music: "Eleanor" by The Turtles. It stops a few minutes into the scene

Jack tends the bar. Sarah is dancing. Elston sits at the bar. He wears an ill-fitting tuxedo. His hair is slicked back. He looks ridiculously out of place. He watches Sarah dance. She's having a great time, singing and dancing all by herself. Jack also watches her dance. Eventually, Sarah winds her way over to Elston. She performs for him, lip-synching to the tune. She runs her hands over the lapels of his tux. She's playful and not at all sexually suggestive. Elston pays her no mind. It's as if she isn't there. Unable to get a response from Elston, Sarah gives up. She sits at the bar and smokes

Sarah They wrote that song about me. Did you know that, Jack?

Jack shrugs

I wasn't even born at the time. But it's about me, anyway. The guy who wrote it, he had a dream of the most fantastic woman he'd ever meet and it was me. How I look now. Did anybody ever write a song about you, Jack?

Jack shrugs

Yeah. So. This guy, he's a Brit and he breaks out in sweats over his dream and so he writes this song. And his buddies in the band, they say, well bloody great, kid. But what's her name? So he says, dunno. Eleanor. Maybe. Then my mother fucks the whole deal and names me Sarah. Right? So. Ten years ago maybe, I'm listening to the radio and I hear this song and I know it's all about me. And I'm freaking out because, Jesus, I know it's the song I'm born to hear. I write the guy a letter, you know, send him a picture. I write, hey, I'm Eleanor but my name's Sarah and I hope you'll understand. The bastard never wrote back. I heard he was dead. Serves him right. But you know, then it gets really creepy. You know what happened then, Jack?

Jack shrugs

I'm at this Springsteen concert, I don't know, five years back, right? And this geezer comes up to me. I mean, this guy's so old his skin is yellow and he wheezes. Got real long hair. Yellow-white. And he grabs me, you know? Strong. For an old bag. And his breath, oh man, it was like ... dirt. Heavy. Like overwhelming ... grime. I think he wants to touch me or, I don't know, something. And he leans in real close and whispers, "Eleanor. How lovely to see you again". Creepy, right? Well. What do you think of that, Jack?

Jack shrugs

I'm thinking maybe I should write it up for a magazine.
Elston Jack be nimble. Jack be quick.

Jack and Sarah consider this

Jack You wanna drink, mister?
Elston (*to Sarah*) Jack be nimble, Jack be quick. It's from a song. "The Limbo Rock".
Sarah Uh-huh. Yeah. So?
Elston A lyric. (*He sings*) "Jack be nimble, Jack be quick. Jack jump ..." I don't remember the rest of it exactly. But it's a song. About Jack. It's fate.
Sarah Wait. Are you saying that somebody wrote a song about Jack? And that it's fate?
Elston No. I'm saying that your meeting with the geezer was fate.
Jack I've never heard this song you're talking about.
Elston I'm saying that the geezer was affirming your belief. Fate.
Sarah Yeah. Well. Maybe he thought I was his long lost granddaughter, too.
Elston It's possible. But not likely. Consider the statistics. In a group of one hundred women, what are the odds that even one of them will be called Eleanor?
Sarah I don't really know. What do you think, Jack?
Jack Dunno. Unless you was sitting in a room full of Roosevelts, I'd have to say the odds would be pretty low.
Elston Exactly.
Sarah Course, maybe there was a run on the name after the song came out. There's lots of Eleanors. Eleanor Parker. Eleanor Rigby.
Jack Eleanor Connolly.

Beat

My ex.

Elston Jack, if I am remembering correctly, and I am not at all sure that I am, Chubby Checker sang "The Limbo Rock".

Sarah So what are you saying? Some old creep with bad breath calls me Eleanor and this means there's UFOs hiding out in a barn in Nebraska?

Elston I'm saying you believe. In fate. In the notion that nothing is random.

Sarah Right. And we're getting looped in some shit hole on the West Side Highway 'cause we knew we were gonna do it and so that's why we're here.

Elston You believe the song was written about you. Fact?

Sarah Yeah. It was.

Elston And you said that your meeting with the geezer was ... creepy? Is that what you called it?

Sarah Yeah. Creepy. Like you.

Elston In my book, Sarah, creepiness is a synonym for what we are afraid to recognize as our own. The very things we ought to embrace but will not. Embrace it. Sarah.

Sarah Uh-huh. Well. What do you think this guy does, Jack?

Jack Dunno. Suit don't fit him.

Sarah Yeah. Like he got lost on his way to a New Year's Eve party a billion years ago. You a fan of *The Twilight Zone*, Jack?

Jack Oh sure. Love the one where that kid wishes everybody into a cornfield. I like that.

Sarah Oh God I wish I could do that. Wish people into cornfields. My boyfriend. My mother. This ... creepy ... guy.

Elston Don't you like my clothing? I wore it for you.

Sarah You hear that, Jack? This fuck wore a monkey suit for me.

Elston I usually don't talk this much. You must be special.

Sarah Your technique's a little creaky. Try again.

Jack Mister. You wanna buy Sarah a drink?

Elston No. She drinks too much. I've noticed.

Jack You wanna buy me a drink? 'Cause if you don't buy somebody a drink I'm gonna have to ask you to leave.

Elston I'm sorry. I mean no disrespect. I'll drink whatever you give me. Please.

Jack You wanna beer?

Elston Whatever you like.

Jack Jack Daniels?

Elston It doesn't matter.

Jack Come on, guy. What? Whiskey sour? Gin tonic? Decide.

Elston I trust you, Jack.

Jack Oh fuck me. I get one customer and he's a wacko faggot.

Elston There's no need to get touchy, Jack.

Sarah Don't mind Jack. He calls everybody a faggot. It's a term of endearment. Some kinda Irish thing. I know. My mother's the same way.

Elston Are you Irish, Sarah?

Sarah Yeah. What are you?

Elston I'm an entertainment attorney.

Jack Look. I don't care what you are. Just order.

Elston All right. A Stoly Martini. Olives.

Sarah A real lawyer drink. A real ... creepy ... lawyer drink.

Elston Why do you say that, Sarah?

Sarah What's an entertainment attorney doing in a dive?

Elston A little bird told me you'd be here.

Sarah You're so full of shit it's coming through your shoes. What are you really? Pimp? Truck driver? Atomic scientist?

Elston I'm an entertainment attorney. Got lots of clients. You ever been to Ireland, Sarah?

Sarah Who are your clients? Name them.

Elston Ireland is beautiful, Sarah. I've been there fifteen times. On business.

Sarah Your client list. Give it to me.

Elston Business takes a man places. Do you know what it's like to be in business, Sarah? Do you know what it's like to travel?

Beat

I have many clients. The Turtles. For instance.

Sarah You're lying.

Elston (*singing*) "Eleanor, gee I think you're swell ..." coincidence? Or fate?

Jack You manage turtles?

Sarah Shut up, Jack. (*To Elston*) Go on. I'm listening.

Elston There's nothing more to say. I'll finish my drink and be gone. If you'd like, I'll send you a couple of tickets to their next concert.

Sarah Nah. I'm kinda busy. And I have a fear of flying. But thanks, you know, for asking.

Elston I'll leave you my card. If you change your mind.

He gives Sarah a business card

Sarah Timothy J Creighton. Entertainment attorney. Yeah. Sure.

Elston You shouldn't doubt me, Sarah. Sarah Casey.

Sarah How'd you know that?

Elston Coincidence. Or fate.

Sarah Yeah. Well. That's not my name. So much for conspiracy theories.

Jack Who said something about conspiracies?

Sarah SHUT UP, JACK. (*To Elston*) All right. Out with it. What do you want?

Elston They call this Hell's Kitchen.

Sarah Great. A tourist.

Elston No. I ... I live on the East Side. I was walking. I like to walk. At night. I like the river. I was thirsty. I stopped.

Sarah You like to drink.

Elston I like to drink.

Sarah And you don't really like to talk. But you talk to me because I'm special.

Elston Yes. And you have kind eyes.

Sarah And I bet you think I have a big heart, right?

Elston Yes.

Sarah A big-hearted hooker. Is that what you think? Guess what. I'm not. Do you understand that? Do you think he understands that, Jack?

Jack shrugs

Elston I don't think you're a hooker. I think you're kind.

Sarah This is where I live, OK? I have a job. You think there's nobody decent living on this side of town? Is that it? Because you are wrong. I'm not some lonely piece of ass losing myself in a booze-bag joint. I'm not.

Elston I'm sorry you're so defensive.

Sarah And I am not impressed by your business card Mr Timothy J Creighton. Are you, Jack?

Jack Nah. See lots of his type. Skinny. Lip sores.

Sarah Creepy looking bastard liar who looks as much like a lawyer as I do a brain surgeon.

Elston All right. I'll tell you what I really do. I kill people.

Jack No shit. For a living?

Elston No. I just kill.

Jack You don't get paid for it?

Elston No. I do it. That's all.

Jack Sonofabitch. How many people you pop?

Elston Six. Maybe seven.

Jack You're not sure?

Elston I'm not certain that one died. She might have lived.

Jack Yeah? Where you been doing this killing?

Elston Here. Upstate. Different places. I like here best.

Jack Yeah. More of a selection, right?

Elston That's right. And anonymity. It's important.

Jack Sure it is. Where do you do them? In the street? Just like that?

Elston No. I take them home. And then I do them. In my apartment. I tend to keep them alive for a few days. Before.

Jack Oh. I get it. Like you're fattening them up and stuff. Yeah.

Elston No. I don't feed them. I talk to them. For a while. Before.

Jack OK. And then. Then what? You ... shoot them?

Elston I drown them. In my bathtub. They put up terrific struggles. I love to watch them fight. You ever drown anyone, Jack?

Jack I drowned a mouse once. Took a fuck of a long time.

Elston Yes. And people take a fuck of a long time, too.

Jack Uh-huh. And I guess this entertainment lawyer shit, I guess you just made that up.

Elston No. There is a Timothy J Creighton and he is an entertainment attorney. Although I'm quite certain he doesn't represent The Turtles.

Jack So this, uh, suit. It ain't yours?

Elston No. It's his.

Jack And you just took it, right?

Elston I borrowed it. I manage a thrift shop. Many people dropping off many clothes and other ... belongings. I have regular customers.

Jack OK. I get it. You put on some other guy's old gear and then you go out and whack girls. Makes sense.

Elston Exactly my point, Jack. I am Mr Creighton when I wear his clothing. I am exceeding wealthy and I live on East Seventy-Fifth Street. My wife is called Rachel and we are fond of making trips to the Cape. But Mr Creighton is compelled to kill people. Coincidence. Or fate?

A tense beat. Elston breaks out into a broad smile. Jack laughs

So. How about another Stoly Martini, Jack. And whatever our friend Sarah would like.

Jack I gotta hand it to you, mister. You had me going there right at the end. Jeez, that part about the clothes. You know, it's like, it's ——

Elston Creepy?

Jack Bet your ass. Jeez. Wow. I'm a fucking sucker.

Elston Fucking faggot sucker.

Jack (*laughing*) Yeah. Fucking faggot sucker. *Salut.*

Sarah So what's your name. Really.

Beat

Elston Tim. Tim Creighton.

Sarah OK. Tim Creighton or whoever you really are. I gotta be up real early tomorrow and I'm so mad at my boyfriend I'm gonna take a hatchet to his face. I'll leave you here with Jack. You can trade stupid jokes and then maybe you can make him your first male victim. As for me, I got to get some sleep. Some of us work day jobs.

Elston What do you do, Sarah?

Sarah I'm a linebacker for the Giants. Satisfied?

Elston No, really. I'm interested in the way you live.

Sarah I bet you are. How about if I told you I'm a prison guard at Rikers Island? While I'm beating the inmates I have fantasies about replacing Sybil Danning in films like ... *Prison Dames in Heat.* Yeah. Sarah Casey, muscles of steel, stars in *Babes Behind Bars.*

Elston So your name is Casey. Sarah Casey. I guessed your name. Fate.

Sarah So what. Some creeps are lucky.

Jack She works in a travel agency.

Sarah Shut up, Jack.

Jack It's her uncle's shop. Down on East Seventh Street. Sells Warsaw package deals to old Pollacks.

Sarah You're disgusting, Jack.

Elston That must be nice for you, Sarah. Working as a travel agent.

Sarah Yeah. I'm thrilled.

Elston Your boyfriend. What's his name?

Sarah Who knows. I used to go with Jack, here. But then I discovered he was an idiot savant. His talent is pouring beer. He's real good at it. But I figure, see, there's no future in it. Jesus. I gotta get out of this city. I'll be brain dead, I keep hanging with crap like you two.

Elston You're a smart girl, Sarah. You'd like to travel. You dream of fame. Fortune. It's out there.

Sarah Listen, asshole. I can play the tough broad with a minimal amount of brains as well as the next girl. And that's fine. That's just ... fine. For people like you.

Elston And why is that fine?

Sarah It's what you expect. Young tart parks her ass on a barstool on Forty-Eighth and the highway. You think, sure, she's fair game. Nice girl. Not too much upstairs. Has a way with men and hairspray. I play along because there's no investment in you. I tell you nothing. You get ... nothing. I remain intact. Yes. I work in my uncle's travel agency while I attend night classes at some second-rate city college. Yes. I dream of many things and no, I am not deluded by unreasonable expectations of a future dazzling life.

Elston And yet you believe that a man who lived several thousand miles away wrote a song about you before you were even born.

Sarah Yeah. And you drown women in your bathtub. We're a couple of charmers, aren't we?

Elston You have kindness. You do. Sarah Casey.

Sarah Thank you. Thanks for the booze, Jack. I'm outta here.

Elston Do you really think I look ridiculous?

Sarah (*considering this*) Absolutely.

Elston I know I do. I dress this way because it's the only way people pay attention to me. Normally, I recede. Like Jack's hairline.

Sarah You're a pretty funny guy, Mr Timothy J Creighton.

Elston You're the only woman who's talked to me.

Sarah You're a sad man, right?

Elston Lonely.

Sarah Oh. That, too. And I'd guess you collect things. What? What do you collect?

Elston Stickpins. Gloves. Spectacles. Accessories. The trappings of things.

Beat

And you don't collect anything. You go to the movies.

Sarah Romantic comedies are my specialty.

Elston Boy gets girl. Boy loses girl.

Sarah Boy cries. Those are my favourites.

Elston And then?

Sarah And then. One night at a shitty rock concert, a dirty old maniac mistakes the girl for somebody he once fucked in a brothel. He calls her Eleanor. She finds it all very creepy. She goes home and passes out. She gets up the next morning. And the next. And maybe the next. That's all. The end.

Jack I never saw a movie like that.

Elston Shut up, Jack.

Jack Hey. Fuckface. Don't you dare tell me to shut up.

Sarah Jack was a Golden Gloves champ.

Jack Fuck me, yes. Light heavyweight. Won twice. Subnovice and open classes.

Sarah He could have been a contender.

Jack Fuck me, yes. I was a contender.

Sarah Of course, Jack was going to be a cop. But. It didn't quite work out. He lost his hair, instead. We're old friends.

Jack Family friends.

Elston You have a large family, Jack?

Jack The largest. Yeah.

Elston I'm an orphan. I was raised in a void.

Sarah Weren't we all. It's late, boys.

Elston But it's not too late for you to talk with me. Sit a while.

Sarah Nope. The early bird gets the worm, et cetera.

Elston You're an early bird. A kind bird.

Sarah I'm really not so kind. I'm not.

Elston I know. That's why I like you. Sit with me. Call me Tim. And I'll call you Eleanor.

Sarah Why?

Elston Because you deserve it.

Beat

I'll tell you stories.

Sarah What kind of stories?

Elston True stories.

Sarah And will they be sad stories?

Elston If you'd like.

Sarah Do you know any UFO stories?

Jack There's this UFO that landed in somebody's backyard in Maine. It lands in the backyard and gets caught up in a clothesline. And all the clothes get caught up, you know, overalls and stuff, 'cause it's the backyard of farmers, so there's lots of denim.

Sarah This is not a true story, Jack.

Jack I swear it's true. And these people, these farmers, they come running out and all their clothes are like, electrified. Electric current's running through their overalls and underwear and it's like watching a moving neon beer sign, you know, a blue one? Oh Jesus, says this one farmer, we got to do something about this shit. And while he's scratching his head wondering what he's gonna do, the electricity eases off and this farmer notices that all his clothes have turned white. The UFO's sucked all the colour from his clothes. Then, he hears music. Violins and shit coming from the UFO.

Sarah Who told you this?

Jack Wait. So. This little fat guy smoking a cigar comes out of the UFO and he says to the farmer, he says: "Upon this rock you will build my church". Then, the fat guy blows smoke at the farmer and disappears. Poof. Just like that. So. The farmer uses the UFO as a church, builds an altar and some pews inside, like, 'cause he goes inside and it's completely empty. No controls. No gears. No nothing. And there it sits until this day. He kept the clothesline up, the one with all the white clothes, as proof. The farmer's got a cable TV show, too.

Sarah You're an asshole, Jack.

Jack It's the truth. State police even found the fat guy's cigar stub. They keep it at the local stationhouse. Framed in glass. It's evidence.

Elston We like evidence, don't we, Jack?

Jack Sure. It's like ... proof. That stuff happened.
Sarah Stuff happens all the time to you, Jack. And you couldn't prove it.
Stupid fuck. If somebody walked in here and levitated you'd probably
claim he was Saint Anthony.
Jack I'm religious. It ain't natural for men to walk on air.
Sarah They don't.
Elston Some men walk on air.
Sarah Yeah? Tell me about it. Tim. Tell me a story about a man who walks
on air.
Elston I shall. Sit a while. Sit.

SCENE 2

A press conference

Jack speaks to the audience. He squints, as if he's under hot bright lights

Jack OK. You guys ready with the light? Right. So where was we? Oh. Yeah.
So there we was, the perp and me. Eyeball to eyeball. Me and the
perpetrator of the alleged aforementioned crime. And I told Sarah, I said,
look woman: this guy ain't kosher. He's like some weirdo in a waiter's
outfit trying to pass himself off as a representative of the legal profession.
But she was real big on him. Impressed by his clothes and his business card,
which, the perp had told us was borrowed. I knew right off. I knew this guy
was a killer. He told us he was. And I take people at their word. I'm a smart
guy. And he wasn't pulling nothing over my eyes. But Sarah, well, she
always had a weakness for little men. Not me. Like I said, I knew right off.
Let me tell you something. This guy had these like ... little sprouts of hair
growing out of his lip. And you gotta figure that's bad news. You figure,
a guy around, what is he? Thirty, forty? And he can't grow facial hair?
What is that? That's like ... bad hormones. It's shit. It's ... perverted. Also,
I gotta tell you about his ears. This friend of mine, he's seen a lot of weird
stuff in certain areas of the Northeast Corridor, and he told me about killer
ears. I swear, yes, there is such a thing. All killers got the same ears. A
German doctor did a study on thirty or forty of them. Guys like Speck, who
popped off the nurses in Chicago. And Berkowitz. You know, the wacko
who killed at the command of a dog? Oh man, whattya gonna say about a
guy who takes orders from a fucking Labrador? So. They got these little
tiny ears. No lobes. Like that Nimoy guy from *Star Trek*. Well, they all got
ears like that, only less pointy. And this German doctor proved that all
killers have these ears. Look it up. It's evidence. It's all ... fucked up. This
Creighton character, he had those ears. I noticed straight off. But I didn't

say nothing 'cause, well, maybe he wasn't. A killer. But was I afraid of him? Nah. Not me. I warned Sarah. I told her. And now it's her own fault she's up and disappeared. Women don't listen. Women don't wait. Sarah and me, we go way back. I'm all broke up, but whattya gonna do? Life proceeds. I won two Golden Gloves. Did I tell you that? I won. Twice.

SCENE 3

Ellen's railroad apartment, Hell's Kitchen

Ted Mitchell sits with Ellen

Ellen Or some ice-cream. I got that. Wouldja like some vanilla, Officer?
Ted No, ma'am. I'm here to ask you things.
Ellen Which things?
Ted Things. About Sarah.
Ellen I told you what I know. She didn't say much. Not a talkative type. Worked downtown in my brother's travel agency. Talked about getting her own place. Never got around to it. She was twenty-five. We had our problems. I can show you pictures of her when she was little.
Ted Mrs Casey. Did Sarah mention any friends, male friends? Was she ... did she have lots of boyfriends?
Ellen What are you implying? Just what are you saying about my Sarah?
Ted Nothing. I want some background is all.
Ellen Sarah had a fella. Skinny little guinea bastard. Anthony. I hated him. She did, too. You talk to him? Go ahead. My Sarah, she had shitty taste but she was faithful. My daughter was no slut.
Ted I never implied she was. Your daughter is missing, Mrs Casey, and it is my obligation to uncover every lead, no matter how trivial or unpleasant.
Ellen She's dead.
Ted We don't know that.
Ellen You have kids, Officer? You got girls?
Ted I have sons.
Ellen You don't worry about boys. Girls, well, they're easier to talk to but you worry. Not that Sarah and me talked. We hardly talked at all. She was moody. She went to night school. What could I say to her? You think about all these things and you don't say any of them and then your kid dies.
Ted There is no evidence that your daughter is dead, ma'am. Please. Talk to me. The contents of her room, was there anything missing? A scrap of paper with a telephone number. Anything.
Ellen There's a single bed with an extra firm mattress and a burnt sienna

crocheted blanket which I made for Sarah when she was twelve and a half. She asked for burnt sienna because she thought it was the saddest colour in the whole Crayola box. It looked good on that *Eyewitness News* telecast, didn't it? Are you sure you don't want some ice-cream?

Ted I'm sure. Thank you.

Ellen Well, that's it. For her room, I mean. Oh yeah. There's a desk with nothing in it. And the record.

Ted What kind of record?

Ellen You saw it when you looked around with your friends. The one that's nailed to the wall. She bought it years ago. Wore out the grooves from playing it so much so she broke it in half. Then she felt so guilty about breaking it, she taped the damned thing back together and nailed it to the wall. Over her bed. She actually thought it was alive, that record. Told me some foreigner wrote the song for her. You think that's a nice thing for a mother to hear? She didn't do no drugs, but she was crazy. If they'd a had therapy when she was a kid, I woulda sent her.

Ted I have two sons, Mrs Casey. And I do worry about them. I know how you feel. And I'd be alarmed, too, if this had happened to either of them. I'm a parent. I sympathize.

Ellen I'm not alarmed. I'm grieving.

Ted That's ... perfectly reasonable given the circumstances, but we haven't the facts ——

Ellen Facts? I don't give a shit about facts. I know what I know. And I know things. In my gut. Like I know my Sarah is gone. Lost to me and to this fucking life she coulda had. I hear her calling. Calling to me. But it's from someplace far away enough so you can hear but you cannot touch. You know what I feel like? I feel like bowling. Heaving a big ball down an alley and having a bunch of big guys throwing their big balls down the alley next to mine. I wanna make a bunch of noise. Lots of noise so I can drown out the sound of my kid calling out to me.

Ted We're doing what we can.

Ellen You know what she's saying to me? She says, "Ma, why'd you have to be such a fucking lousy parent." Over and over. Just that one thing. Well. She wasn't much of a talker.

Beat

Maybe you'll be wanting some of that ice-cream now, huh?

SCENE 4

A travel agency, Lower East Side

Sarah is behind the counter. Elston is at the counter. He wears glasses and sports a moustache

Sarah I'm sorry, mister ...
Elston Jonas. Mr Paul Jonas.
Sarah Yes. Mr Jonas. There really aren't any junkets to Siberia.
Elston I didn't think there would be. But I figured, hey, it's worth a try. It's a hard place to get to. By yourself. I thought maybe a group, maybe there'd be a group of people who shared my curiosity about the place. I'm very curious about Siberia. Aren't you?
Sarah I guess I am. Curious. About different places.
Elston But not about Siberia?
Sarah No. Not really. I'm sorry.
Elston That's OK. You're honest. I like that in a travel agent. So many agents trying to sell you so many packages. So many bad packages. They'll sell you anything for a commission. And with so many people travelling these days. So many Americans travelling.
Sarah Uhm. Yes.
Elston Business must be good for you.
Sarah Fairly good. Yes. So. You've got, let me see if this is right. You've got four weeks and you would like to go ——
Elston Someplace cold. And distant.
Sarah Cold and distant. I see.
Elston Well, because of heat-stroke.
Sarah You don't do well in heat. I understand.
Elston Oh, no. No, no, no. It's not me I'm worried about. I'm very healthy. It's others who worry me. I can't bear seeing people succumbing to the effects of heat. I'm queasy. You go somewhere cold, you don't have to put up with that sort of thing.
Sarah That's true. Perhaps Europe. It's off season. Rates are very low. Austria's beautiful.
Elston Really? Have you ever been there?
Sarah Well, actually no. I myself, I have never been to Austria. But my clients have told me. And of course, I've seen photographs.
Elston There'd be skiing accidents. Broken bones. You'd have to consider that.
Sarah I'm not following you, Mr Jonas.
Elston In Austria. Mountains. Skiing.

Sarah But you wouldn't have to ski. Not necessarily.

Elston Good point. Chances are, though, that I'd *see* an accident. Mountains everywhere. I'd be surrounded.

Sarah Well. There are cities. Vienna, for instance. I don't think there are any mountains in Vienna. Not within city limits.

Elston It's intensely clean there, isn't it?

Sarah I think I've heard that.

Elston You can't trust a place that clean. You live in a filthy place, you can't ever really get used to a sparkling clean place, can you?

Sarah I guess not.

Elston Have you ever tried? To live in a clean place?

Sarah I've lived in New York all my life. I suppose that means I've lived in filth and filth alone.

Elston Well, I tried. Once I moved to Utah. The salt lake's out there. But Utah was religious. And I don't trust that, either. Religious peoples harbour the strangest notions, don't you think? Especially Mormons. And Catholics. Are you Catholic?

Sarah Yes. As a matter of fact.

Elston I could tell by your name. Casey. Good Catholic name. My wife says I snoop. I'm sorry. Tell me if I snoop. My wife, she would like to go someplace warm that has a casino. She likes to gamble. But me, I like to sit and shiver.

Sarah How about if I could find you someplace cold. With a casino. Best of both worlds, no?

Elston My wife's name is Natasha. She's not Russian. But she has a Russian name. I find that odd. Her father's favourite writer was Dostoevsky and he believed he was naming her after a character. I have a joke with Natasha. If we ever have a kid, we promise to call it Raskolnikov.

Elston laughs. Sarah doesn't

Elston Raskolnikov. Get it? *Crime and Punishment.* The book.

Sarah I've heard of it.

Elston Dostoevsky wrote it, see? It's about ... well, here I go babbling. Babble, babble. That's what I do. I'm so limited in what I can say to other people at my own job that I just ... go overboard with anybody else I meet. Sorry. I'm a bankruptcy trustee.

Sarah That's ... really interesting.

Elston Oh, but it's not. It's heart-breaking. I take things away from people in order to provide them with a false sense of renewal. When you take something from somebody, it stays took. They don't understand that. I do.

Beat

How about Alaska? You been there?

Sarah No. I haven't. However ... it is cold. And there might be gambling.

Elston Bingo halls. Of course. Eskimo bingo parlours. Or perhaps I'm thinking of the Indians.

Beat

You're very well-spoken. For a travel agent.

Sarah Thanks. I guess.

Elston It's a gift. Take me, for example. Here I am, chirp chirp chirping away at you, and I don't consider myself to be particularly adept at the gift of the gab.

Sarah It's ... I'm in a people job.

Elston Hmmm. But then, so am I. Difference being that in your people job, you give them things. Information, accommodation. The potential for snapshots. Me, I remove things from people. Information, accommodation. Cash.

Sarah Mr Jonas. Have you decided on a European vacation this year?

Elston Oh. Oh, I am sorry. I think I'm being gracious but what I really am is a fool.

Sarah I didn't mean that. Time. That's all. Time's a-wasting.

Elston Oh, yes. I understand. Tick tock. Miss Casey. The most well-spoken travel agent I've ever met. But you're not well-travelled, are you?

Sarah Well. No. I'm not ... well-travelled.

Elston Gosh. That's really strange. I mean, how can you sell airline tickets if you've never been on an airplane?

Sarah I've been on airplanes. I have. But. It's true, I've never been abroad.

Elston Would you like to go abroad?

Sarah Yes. Very much. I'd like to see ... Winchester.

Elston An odd place for a young person to choose.

Sarah Well, you know, there's that song. You know. (*Singing*) "Winchester Cathedral, you're bringing me ——"

Elston You have a lovely singing voice, Miss Casey.

Sarah Oh God, no. I don't. But thanks.

Elston Do you sing in the shower?

Sarah Pardon?

Elston I do. Secret singers. Singing in showers. I sing Yma Sumac in the shower. Who do you sing?

Sarah I ... sing along. To different songs. There's this bar I go to. You know, a neighbourhood place in the Forties, near the highway and ——

Elston East or West?

Sarah What?

Elston Direction. Direction is important in travel. Precision. So. There's a neighbourhood bar in the Forties. East or West?

Sarah West. On the highway, actually.

Elston Of course. Sorry. Don't mind me. I'm an interrupter. By nature.

Sarah Yeah. So. That's where I sing. In this bar. Sometimes I think it's open only for me to wander in and sing. Hardly anybody else goes there. Just me and Jack, he's the owner. I mean, sometimes a bum'll wander in and I give him a candy bar. Or something.

Elston You're a kind soul.

Sarah Nah. I just like to see people once in a while. People I don't know.

Elston But in your job, you see people you don't know all the time.

Sarah It's different. Here I talk about departures and arrivals. At the bar, I talk about ... singing. Drinking. You know.

Elston I do know. It must be sad having a job where there's no psychic stability. Always coming or going. Never staying put. The travel motif.

Sarah Oh, sure. And you know what? When I'm in the bar with Jack and I listen to the tunes — he's got a really nice old Wurlitzer, only plays sixties tunes? Sixties tunes are the best, 'cause I know I was meant to be my age now, except I was meant to be my age in the sixties. Once, I woke up and I knew all the lyrics to all songs written in the nineteen sixties. Creepy.

Elston Yes. I see.

Sarah And I think, hey Sarah, whatcha doing being alive in the nineties? You missed the boat, girl. There's no going back. And then I get sad.

Elston I find it interesting, metaphorical perhaps, that you work here. If you're around travellers enough, you'll become one yourself. And travel right back into the nineteen sixties.

Sarah Well. Not exactly. Christ, no. Don't get me wrong. I'm basically a happy person. I got a job. I gotta boy. Anthony. He's sweet but he's dumb. Big hearted. A hairdresser.

Elston Got a.

Sarah What?

Elston Got a. Not gotta. Enunciation, Miss Sarah Casey.

Beat

I like that phrase. Its implications. Christ, no.

Sarah Yeah. Whatever.

Beat

It's time. We picked a place. For you and your wife.

Elston I hope you don't mind me correcting you.
Sarah No. No, you're right.
Elston It's just that you're so well-spoken. Generally.
Sarah Absolutely. I should ... pay attention. To things. Like that.
Elston So. Let's see. Where to go? You pick.
Sarah I can't do that. It's your vacation.
Elston But you've been such a help already. And I don't especially care where I go. What's important is the travel itself. Here. I've brought this.

Elston gives Sarah a map

Sarah It's a map of the New York metropolitan area. New Jersey. Connecticut.
Elston Well. There is the theory that the closer one stays to home, the further one actually travels. Emily Dickinson.
Sarah What about her?
Elston She proves the theory. She never left home. But she travelled. Frequently. (*He points to the map*) Pick a place. Go on. Close your eyes and let your fingers do the walking.
Sarah You know, if I do that, you might wind up in some truly awful place.
Elston A vacation is what you make of it. A snapshot of a landfill can be just as rewarding as a snapshot of the Eiffel Tower.

A long beat, then Sarah closes her eyes and picks a place on the map. She opens her eyes, and she and Elston ponder her choice

Seems I'm to spend my vacation in the Holland Tunnel.
Sarah I could pick again.
Elston Please don't. I believe in fate. And not in coincidence. Don't you?

SCENE 5

Natalie's apartment, Upper East Side

Elston is dressed as he was in Scene 1. He holds out a box of chocolates to Natalie

Elston It's Fannie Farmer. Sorry. I meant to bring something else. But things weren't open. This being Sunday.
Natalie I love chocolate, Elston. Thank you.
Elston It's embarrassing, though. Even I know it's cheap chocolate.
Natalie Well. It's the thought that counts.

Elston doesn't give Natalie the chocolate; she clocks this

Elston Yes.
Natalie How's the shop? I know I haven't been around lately but ... this cold.
  Can't seem to shake it.
Elston It's the time of year. For colds.
Natalie Yes. Yes, it is.

Beat

  So. The shop. It's doing well?
Elston It's heavy on donations. Will you allow me to take you to dinner?
Natalie No. Thank you. I have plans.
Elston You're the kind of person who has plans. I'm not.
Natalie Oh, I don't have too many plans. I go with the flow.
Elston I wish I could go with the flow. But I can't. I read too much.
Natalie Well. Reading's ... a good thing. To do.
Elston I mean, I'm not criticizing my job. You were kind to give me work.
  But it's not a fast-paced environment. I don't mind. I have time to read.
  Magazines. Trade magazines. You would not believe the number of
  different professions out there, Natalie. And each profession has a trade
  magazine. Why do you suppose they're called trade magazines?
Natalie Look. I really don't know.
Elston There's no barter system involved. It's not like, I trade you money
  for clothes. It's all about taking. Not trading. Don't you think?
Natalie You're absolutely right, Elston. It's all about taking. So. How about
  I take the week's receipts from you?
Elston Laura sends her best.
Natalie Great. Send her mine.
Elston Wouldn't you like to meet her? I mean, she knows how much you've
  done for me. She admires you.
Natalie Meeting Laura would be ... nice. Sometime.
Elston We're going to be married. In the fall. I saw a travel agent two weeks
  ago and arranged the trip. We're going through the Holland Tunnel. By car.
  I wish we could take a train, though. I love trains. And people who travel.
  Don't you?
Natalie When you work, it's hard to travel.
Elston But you don't work. You own.
Natalie Still. I've got to keep an eye on things, don't I?
Elston Do you feel you've got to keep an eye on me?
Natalie No. That is not what I meant. I mean to say that ownership is a great
  responsibility.

Elston I see what you mean. Like the slaves. That was a great responsibility, keeping an eye on so many people.

Natalie The receipts. Give me the receipts, Elston.

Elston Laura's on tour this week. That's why I have a free night and why I thought you might ... she's a tennis player. Did I tell you that?

Natalie You might have. I don't really remember.

Elston She's never won a tournament but she's in constant motion. I love athletes, don't you? Such grace under pressure. Such skill. I am completely unskilled. Have you ever noticed that about me?

Natalie Yes. Yes, I ... no. I didn't mean to suggest ——

Elston Laura's a pretty girl. Tall. Taller than me. A redhead. Freckles. Thin ankles. I like that in a woman. The kind of ankle that looks like it would break if you so much as blow on it. We were high school sweethearts. In Idaho. She was the prom queen. I wasn't the king. But she preferred me to all the others. I was in science club. I looked at things. Under slides. Glass makes things look better. If people walked around pressed between two gigantic slides of glass, they'd look better, too.

Natalie ELSTON. (*Beat*) Please. The receipts. I need the receipts.

Elston gives Natalie a large envelope. Natalie looks through it

This is good, Elston. Very neat. You've done well this week. Thank you.

Elston Natalie is a beautiful name.

Natalie Well, yes. It is. Thank you.

Elston A real spy name. My wife Natasha has a spy name and I'm forever telling her ——

Natalie What? What did you say?

Elston I was saying. I was. My sister. She's ... never mind.

Natalie You said your wife. Natasha.

Elston Did I? I'm thinking of Laura. Would you possibly travel with me?

Natalie I think you should leave now. I have plans.

Elston I feel the urge to have plans. Let's travel to dinner. I don't know much about you, Natalie, but I would like to know. Everything.

Natalie Our relationship prohibits. It.

Elston Do we have a relationship?

Natalie Yes. I'm your employer. I employ you.

Elston I like that. I work for you. I belong to you.

Natalie I wouldn't go that far.

Elston I meant it figuratively. I love language. Don't you? I'm all dressed up with no place to go. Won't you let me buy you dinner? Let me spend money on you.

A telephone rings. It rings again. A beat

Natalie Excuse me, Elston. Don't touch — just stay put. All right?

Natalie exits

The telephone rings again. And again. Silence

Elston (*as if Natalie is still there*) I'm a magician. Really. Me and a girl named Blue, we do the New England carnival circuit. Did I tell you that? I have a special trick that nobody else does. Let me show you. (*He takes a box of matches out of his pocket. He lights one and holds it between his thumb and forefinger. It burns down to his fingers. He doesn't flinch*) People faint when they see this trick. It doesn't hurt. It never hurts. It never hurts. (*Beat*) I love fire. The way it travels. Don't you? Let me show you another trick. (*He unwraps the box of chocolates. He eats them at a rapid pace, stuffing them into his mouth*) Excess. Excess is my encore. It's astonishing.

Natalie enters. She watches Elston eating the chocolates

(*Noticing her*) I was hungry.
Natalie I'm running late. You'll have to go.
Elston How can you go out on a date if you have a cold you can't shake?
Natalie Watch me and see.
Elston When will you go to dinner with Laura and me?
Natalie Some other time, Ellie. When I don't have any plans.
Elston But you always have plans.
Natalie Yes. I do.
Elston So that means you don't go with the flow. You said you did. Could I ask you for a raise?
Natalie Ask me some other time.
Elston When? When shall I ask you?
Natalie Soon. We'll talk.
Elston We will? Good. Because there are some things I'd like to ask you. For instance, why is it called a thrift shop? Seems to me it ought to be called a generosity shop. You know?
Natalie I'll have to think about that one. Later.
Elston Have you ever been to New Jersey?
Natalie No. And I don't ever want to go. Leave now. Please. I really have to get out ——
Elston Isn't it funny how you can live in a place for years and there's this other place right over a river yet you never seem to get there?

Beat

You called me Ellie. Before. Why'd you do that?

SCENE 6

A press conference

Jack and Ellen speak to the audience, into microphones. Ted and Timothy Creighton watch them

Ellen (*tapping her microphone*) Is this on? Hello, hello. One small step for man, one giant leap for mankind. Testing. One. Two. Three. Hello. Ladies and gentlemen of the press: this is the press conference. With me is Jack Fallon, the bartender who, as far as we know, is the last person to have seen my Sarah before she ... went away. What's that? Well. No. We don't know that she exactly went away.

Jack We sure don't.

Ellen Mr Fallon will now make his statement.

Jack This is my statement: listen, buddy. We want her back. Come back, Sarah. (*Beat*) That's all.

Ellen (*fielding questions*) What's that, miss? Nope. Haven't heard a thing. No ransom notes. And it's a good thing, too, 'cause I ain't got any money. I'm ordinary. YOU HEAR ME, YOU SKINNY CREEP? I GOT NO MONEY.

Beat

I have some pictures of Sarah from happier times. (*She displays some baby photos*) See? All smiles. And to think she might be, at this very moment, stuffed in a trunk or bound and gagged and forced to — well. A mother's private grief is best not spread over the airwaves.

Jack Mrs Casey ain't feeling well, fellas. (*Fielding questions*) What? No. No, I can't talk to you about that night on the advice of the New York City Police Department. Can't give away details of what you might call the perp's *modus operandi*. Huh? No. I ain't got no book deals out of this. And the bar's open, guys. Round the clock. I got my mother working days. Just in case, you know, the asshole's stupid enough to come back. I'm offering my Golden Gloves trophies to anybody who comes into the bar with information leading to the arrest of the perp. How's that?

Ellen I just wanna say: honey, come home. I'm keeping a candle in the window so you can see our satellite antenna guiding your way. Your room is untouched by human hands. Except, you know, mine. I boughtcha a new record. See? (*She holds up a 45rpm record*) Cost a bundle, so you better come back and listen to it. I hoped you was gonna be a nurse so you could patch up the mess I — I can't. I can't go on. The stress. The sleepless nights. What's that? No. I don't got no current pictures of Sarah. We stopped taking pictures when the Polaroid broke. No. No graduation photos. I wasn't there. Look. It wasn't a big deal.

Ted steps forward

Ted Thank you, Mrs Casey. At this time, we'd like to announce that we have located Timothy Creighton, who had been identified as the man with whom Sarah Casey left O'Malley's saloon on the evening of the thirteenth. Mr Creighton would you please step forward?

Timothy, desperately shy and uncomfortable, inches forward. Ellen and Jack watch him

Jack That ain't him.
Ted We know.
Timothy (*at a microphone*) My name is Timothy Creighton. I was not in O'Malley's saloon on the night of the thirteenth. I've never been to O'Malley's saloon. In fact, I've never been west of Fifth Avenue. Nor do I plan an excursion west of Fifth Avenue in the foreseeable future. I am an entertainment attorney. I am forty-three years old. My wife, a research biologist, and my three sons are my pride and joy. I have been, from time to time, a Little League coach. I have never met Sarah Casey and really, I don't plan to meet her. In the foreseeable future. Though, of course, I and my entire family, wish her well and expect that she will return to her ... mother ... soon. I am — I am disturbed. By the incessant media crush I've been subjected to. My doorman, regrettably, has fallen prey to the temptation of easy cash and so several of you have been permitted to camp inside my building's lobby. And my wife swears that some of you have watched her doing laundry in our basement. Thus, Detective Mitchell and I have decided the time is right. For me to come forward. I am not involved in any way in this case. Nor do I know who might be. Please. Leave us alone. Contrary to published reports, I am not part of a satanic ritual abuse cult. I do not make human sacrifices. My wife was never involved in a day care scandal and yes, my children are my own. Let me repeat: I am not a criminal. I'm just ... tired of getting funny looks from my greengrocer. I'm afraid to go to my barber. Please. Understand this. Thank you.

Timothy exits

Ted (*to Ellen and Jack*) He's given us a name.
Jack What name?
Ted A name. Of a man. There might be a connection.
Ellen He seems like such a nice man.
Ted Mrs Casey. We have a lead. A good one.
Ellen Lead? What lead? My daughter's dead. (*Beat, then back to the press corps*) I'm crocheting a new blanket for Sarah so it's ready for her. When she comes home.

SCENE 7

Ellen's apartment

Music: "Paper Doll" by the Mills Brothers. Sarah is dressed as she was in Scene 1. She dances with Anthony, trying to teach him to waltz, but it's really the wrong song to be using. Ellen reads a tabloid

Anthony Hey. Gimme a break, Sarah. This music sucks for dancing.
Sarah It's not so bad. It's old. I like old things.
Anthony Yeah. Like your mother.
Ellen Hey. Shit for brains. Watchya mouth.
Anthony Mrs Casey, you ever dance to this stuff?
Ellen Leave me alone. I'm reading. I'm learning things.
Anthony Yeah? What things?
Ellen Important things.
Sarah Ma. You don't learn anything by reading stuff like that. Read a book. A newspaper.
Ellen I watch TV for my news. I like the colour commentary.
Anthony Mrs Casey, you know how to waltz?
Ellen Sure. Sarah's pig of a father taught me when he was drunk. He thought he was Christopher Plummer and I was Julie Andrews in *The Sound of Music*. He tried to re-enact the gazebo scene. It didn't work. But wouldn't that be nice? A gazebo. I've always wanted one.
Sarah You can't have a gazebo in the city, Ma.
Ellen Why not? People got shrines, don't they? I want a gazebo. Hey Anthony: you gonna buy me a gazebo?
Anthony Yeah. When your daughter marries me.
Sarah Great. Like I'm some fucking dowry for a gazebo.
Ellen Marry him already. Get it over with.
Sarah I'd rather he learned to waltz.
Ellen What? So you can dance at the wedding?

Sarah No. That's not why.
Ellen What the fuck are you talking about? Nobody dances once they're married.
Anthony Hey, Mrs Casey. Watchya mouth.
Ellen You big asshole. Shut up. Cut my hair. Ain't that what you do? Cut hair?
Anthony You want a haircut now?
Ellen Fucking right. Come over here and make me beautiful.

Anthony tends to Ellen's hair throughout the remainder of the scene

Sarah I can't believe this, Anthony. You promised.
Anthony I kept my promise. We danced.
Sarah Don't cut her hair. Let's go out.
Anthony You wanna go to the movies?
Sarah No. I just ... wanna go. Downtown. To the village. I want a double espresso.
Anthony I can make you a double espresso. Besides, you know I don't feel right in those café places. Lotsa guys, you know, talking about foreign films and stuff.
Sarah What's wrong with that?
Anthony Nothing. If you're a foreigner.
Sarah I hate you sometimes, Anthony. I really do.
Ellen A perfect way to enter marriage. With rage. Go on. Do it. I waited until my rage at your father was gone before I married him. And look at what an uninteresting life we led. May he rest in peace.
Sarah I don't want to get married. I want to travel.
Anthony Fine. We'll go to Sicily on our honeymoon. My grandma's got a big house with those french windows.
Sara I don't want to visit your grandmother. I want to visit Italy.
Anthony Sicily's Italy. I speak the language. Don't worry.
Sarah I DON'T LIKE YOUR GRANDMOTHER.
Ellen I'll go with you, Anthony. We get there, you sit me in a garden, give me a jug of red wine, you go off and do your business. I need a vacation.
Sarah Anthony. Come out with me. Now.
Anthony Say you'll marry me and I'll come out with you.
Sarah I don't want to marry you.
Ellen And just who does she think she's gonna marry?
Anthony She's playing hard to get.
Ellen I played hard to get once. And what did it get me? Got me a man who thought he was a member of the Von Trapp family singers. Take a hint from your mother, girlie. Marry this guy. He's got his own business.

Anthony (*to Sarah*) I love you, babe.

Sarah Jesus. Fuck you all. I'm too young to get married.

Ellen You know, Anthony, she's been this way since she's been taking night classes at Pace.

Anthony Yeah? I didn't notice no changes.

Ellen Oh, I notice the changes. She speaks in tongues. You oughtta hear it.

Sarah I'm studying Greek, Ma.

Ellen Yeah, well. Whatever it is, I can't read it. And if I can't read it, cook it or hit it, I don't trust it. Do me a favour, Sarah. Just say you'll marry him.

Anthony We're gonna have a great reception. My brother's band is gonna play. We'll have it at this place out in Flatbush.

Sarah I won't get married in Flatbush.

Ellen What? You'd rather get married here? See, Anthony? I think Sarah has this hunch she's gonna marry some Hollywood type. Kinda guy she can speak in tongues to. But look. Look at what I'm reading. It says that everybody in California is dying from cancer. See? So it don't do you no good to leave home.

Anthony I hadda uncle who went to California. San Diego. There's some kinda really big aquarium and it was his lifelong dream to go there and see the whales. So he saves and saves his money — which he was doing for a long time, cause he was a hot dog vendor at Yankee Stadium — and finally he gets the cash together for the trip. He don't tell nobody he's going, 'cause it's like something he's been dreaming of his whole life and you don't share that stuff with anybody. So one night, he just disappears to San Diego. Turns up at Sea World. And what happens is, the place is closed. The first time in its history the place is closed for renovations. My uncle's, like, booked this two-week trip. So what does he do? Every day for two weeks he leaves his motel and drives to the gates. Stands there all day long. Fucking old guy trying to glimpse a whale through gates.

Sarah I don't want to hear any more stories about life's little disappointments, Anthony.

Ellen Be quiet, you. Go on, Anthony. I like this story. It's soothing.

Anthony You're not gonna believe what happens to him.

Ellen What? Don't tell me. The whale, using an animal's ESP, senses your uncle's presence and swims up to the gates?

Sarah You're sick.

Anthony No, wait. Wait. So. On his last night, he's frantic. He's gotta leave the next morning. And he knows he ain't ever gonna be able to afford the trip again, 'cause, like he's seventy-seven goddamned years old. So. On that last night, he starts climbing the gate, scales it, like he's a teenager or something. He gets to the top and for a single second, I guess he can see the whales. Then, like that: ba-bing. He slips at the edge, impales himself on the top of the gate. Ba-boom. Clean shot. Right through the heart. Poor fuck.

Ellen (*laughing*) At least he didn't stay in California long enough to catch the cancer.

Sarah You two are pathetic. That's a really charming story, Anthony. I guess there's some lesson attached to it? A moral?

Anthony Lesson? Who said anything about a lesson? I'm asking you to marry me, Sarah.

Ellen The lesson is this: don't go nowhere without calling ahead to see if it's open. That means you, Sarah.

Sarah I'm not calling nobody. Europe's always open, Ma. Countries don't close.

Ellen Yes they do. Fucking Russians closed their country.

Sarah Guess what. IT'S OPEN AGAIN. Read something. LEARN SOME-THING.

Ellen Look you little bitch: I know more than you're ever gonna know. You got your father's attitude, oh Miss high and mighty stuck up bastard daughter of a mick NO GOOD FUCK. I know all I need to know about how to get through THINGS.

Anthony Hey hey — chill out, Mrs Casey. I got the scissors right here. Don't wanna hurt you.

Ellen Go ahead. Hurt me. I won't notice. I got a daughter who uses me for a doormat. Wipes her feet all over my GUTS. I'M SORRY I DON'T GOT THE KEYS TO FUCKING PARIS FRANCE IN MY POCKET.

Sarah Anthony, you want to know what I did in school on Friday?

Ellen GO ON. HURT ME. SUE ME.

Sarah Answer me, Anthony.

Anthony Yeah, yeah babe. I do. If I listen to what you did at college, wouldja marry me? Wouldja?

Sarah I'm going out.

Ellen Yeah? Where ya going on a Sunday night?

Sarah I'm going to Russia. There's a train leaving Grand Central any minute.

Beat

I'll be at O'Malley's.

Ellen Oh. Little booze bag.

Sarah Bitch. You make me wanna give up. You hear that? I sit here with the two of you, and you make me want to GIVE UP. I sit here too long and it's like tendrils grow up my legs, like I'm being rooted here.

Ellen That's because you can't communicate. That's because you're moody.

Sarah It's in my genes.

Anthony What's in your jeans, babe? You restless?
Sarah Yeah. I'm restless. I wanna talk to Jack. He always listens.
Ellen And I don't?
Sarah I'll be at O'Malley's.

Beat

Don't wait up.

SCENE 8

A thrift shop, Upper East Side

Elston wears boxer shorts. He's surrounded by clothes, which he sorts through. There's a full-length mirror nearby

Elston (*holding up a pair of trousers*) Thank you, Mr Harris. Thank you for the wool. When it's cold, wool's best. Unless you have cashmere. But who can afford it? Mr Harris, I hope you and your wife are warm tonight. I hope you are huddled together and sipping champagne by candlelight. I hope you have a fireplace. I hope your children are asleep and dreaming of a time when they'll be free to travel. I hope they're never ill. I hope you remember me. (*He puts on the trousers, then holds up a shirt*) And thank you, Mr Chester Ingalls, for this cotton. It's a very fine English shirt. I hope you're in London now. I hope you're relaxing in a five-star hotel in Knightsbridge. I hope you're not afraid of leaving your home after dark. I hope you never tire of giving away your old clothes. I hope you remember me. (*He puts on the shirt, then holds up a jacket*) And where would I be without you, Mr Holloway? This jacket is a magnificent piece of tailoring. The very finest silk and linen. The mixture is exquisite. I fear you're full of rage. I hope you don't beat your girlfriend. I hope she agrees to the house in Westbury. I hope that one day you will hop a commuter train to that house and there she'll be. Waiting for you at the station in a red Volvo. I hope you never declare bankruptcy. I hope you remember me. (*He puts on the jacket and examines himself in the mirror*) For what is a man without his friends?

Ted enters

Ted Elston Rupp?
Elston Yes.
Ted The door was open. The front door.
Elston Yes.

Ted I'm Ted Mitchell. NYPD. Homicide division.
Elston Yes.
Ted I'd like to ask you some questions. Would you ... come with me?
Elston Yes.
Ted Shall we go?
Elston Do you have a car?
Ted Yes. The car's outside. Out front.
Elston I love cars.

Beat

   Take me someplace.

Elston holds his hands out in front of his body, as if to be handcuffed

Black-out

ACT II

A police station, mid-town

Ted is interviewing Elston

Elston Is this the place where you question criminals?
Ted Sometimes.
Elston It looks like that kind of place. I've never been to one of those places. But. This has the feel of a place where people experience fear.
Ted Are you experiencing fear?
Elston Oh, no. No. I trust you. You took me someplace.
Ted You like to travel.
Elston Yes, I do. But I don't often get the chance. Work. Family obligations.
Ted You told me you don't have a family.
Elston That doesn't mean I don't have obligations. To family. We carry obligation with us, Ted. Regardless.
Ted You had family. Once. Tell me about them.
Elston Am I under arrest?
Ted No.
Elston Do you have a family?
Ted Everybody does.
Elston And do you feel obligated to them?
Ted Tell me some more about Sarah Casey.
Elston A lovely girl. A travel agent. Do you know she never went anywhere?
Ted No. I didn't. How do you know that?
Elston She told me.
Ted When? When did she tell you that?
Elston When did you become a detective?
Ted Did Sarah Casey tell you she never travelled before or after you left O'Malley's?

Beat

   I became a detective six years ago.
Elston Did you have to shoot somebody to become a detective?

Ted No, Elston. It doesn't work that way.

Elston Did you have to go to a special school?

Ted No. No special school. Tell me more about Sarah Casey.

Elston Sarah Casey went to school. But she didn't need any particular skills to become a travel agent. Just like you don't need particular skills to be a detective.

Ted I answered some questions for you. Now, you answer some for me.

Elston Give and take. I give, you take. Am I under arrest?

Ted No. Should you be?

Elston I have many friends. Natalie's my best friend.

Ted I know. She told me that.

Elston When did she tell you that?

Ted Oh, about the same time Sarah Casey was telling you about her lack of travel skills.

A silence

Elston Natalie has nice ankles. Did she show you them?

Ted She showed me her ledgers. Said you kept them up well. Said you're a good worker. Solid. Honest. Are you honest?

Elston I'm taking Natalie to dinner next week. She's very busy. But she made time for me.

Ted Did you have dinner with Sarah Casey?

Elston When? When are we talking? I need times. I do better. With a little direction. That's why I'm such a good worker.

Ted That Sunday.

Elston That Sunday.

Beat

No. No dinner with Sarah Casey.

Ted But you did leave O'Malley's with her.

Elston Yes. Yes, I did.

Ted And then?

Elston I went home.

Ted And what about Sarah?

Elston She's lovely. A travel agent. I love to travel. Am I under arrest?

Ted No.

Beat

I love to travel.

Elston Do you? You must drive a lot. Being a detective.

Ted Did you know that the average detective logs more miles per annum than the average cabbie?

Elston Yes. I do know that. Maps. You must have lots of maps.

Ted Oh, sure. I had a special glove compartment built to accommodate all my maps. I like roads.

Elston Yes. And there are many, many roads in this country. Aren't there?

Ted Yup. Roads are necessary for travel. And for what else?

Elston Sight-seeing. Speedy exits.

Ted That's the interesting part. Speedy exits.

Elston You sound like you know what I'm talking about, Ted.

Ted Yes. Fast cars. Starless nights. Blind alleys. Places to hide. Speedy exits.

Elston If you drive so much, you should know what I'm talking about. That's not what I'm talking about.

Ted Educate me, Elston. Please.

Elston I observe speed limits. Actually, I always drive in the right lane. With the old people. Except for the exits. On exit ramps, I accelerate. Fifty, sixty, seventy. Someday I'd like to take an exit ramp at eighty.

Ted Isn't that dangerous?

Elston I don't know. Maybe.

Ted If you think it might be dangerous, then why do you do it?

Elston I get excited when I anticipate arriving. At a destination. Having a family is dangerous, too.

Ted Maybe.

Elston Well. If you think it might be dangerous, then why do you do it?

Ted Do you own a car, Elston? Did you maybe take Sarah Casey for a ride?

Elston I take cabs. I like cabs. Do you know, I won't take a cab unless it has a plexiglass barrier inside to separate passenger and driver?

Beat

I used to drive. But I've never owned a car, Ted.

Ted We've been at this for two hours. Did you know that?

Elston Yes. It's been very pleasant. Did Natalie tell you she didn't like me? Because I wouldn't like to spend money on a woman who doesn't like me.

Ted You like money.

Elston No. I don't. That's why I spend it.

Ted Did you spend any money on Sarah Casey?

Elston Oh, no. I barely know her. Though she likes me. I would spend money on her. She's kind. Are you kind, Ted?

Ted All right, Elston. These are the things I know about you: you like to travel. You won't ride in certain taxis. You're a good worker who keeps an honest ledger. You met Sarah Casey at O'Malley's last Sunday evening. You left the bar with her. You're taking Natalie to dinner. Give me something else. Sarah Casey has disappeared.

Elston Good for her. She deserves to go. Away. She's never been anywhere.

Ted Did you take her anywhere?

Elston Well. I told her that there was the possibility. Of going away.

Ted You have a fiancée named Laura.

Elston Laura is a tennis player.

Ted I know. She's never won a match.

Elston She's never won a tournament.

Ted There's one thing, though, Elston. About Laura. We can't find her.

Elston Perhaps she went away.

Ted We can find no evidence that she actually exists.

Elston You know, Ted, when I was a boy, people went away a lot. And they never came back.

Ted People who go away generally leave a trail.

Elston Are you going to arrest me?

Ted Tell me why you posed as Tim Creighton last Sunday night.

Elston Because I wore his clothes.

Ted You told Jack Fallon and Sarah Casey that you were a killer.

Elston I also told them I was Timothy J Creighton. Ted. Why won't you arrest me?

Ted I will ask you once more. Why. Why did you tell those people you were a killer?

Elston Because they believed me. Because. Haven't you ever wanted to be anybody else, Ted?

Ted Never. Why do you want to be somebody else?

Elston Because I'm more honest than you. I know. Who I actually am. Do you?

Beat

Arrest me. Please.

Ted Are you a killer?

Elston Have you ever shot anyone on the job?

Ted Not yet.

Elston But don't you want to? Don't you? If you don't have an urge to use your gun, why do you carry it? Shoot me.

Ted That's enough. That's — look. I'll tell you something. I admit it. I don't like my job. I don't especially like the company I'm keeping lately. I don't like you. I might be doing other things. I might have swum the English Channel. I might have been a priest.

Elston I wish you were a priest, Ted. I wish I had something to confess.

Ted I really couldn't care less for a confession. I want to believe that you are just another sad bastard who's got a thing for wearing other people's cast offs. I want to believe that you lead the same fucking boring life I lead. That the worst thing you've ever done is short-change Natalie a few bucks on the week's take. Tell me you're dull, Elston. Tell me what I want to hear. Help me see this through.

Elston You're an unhappy man, Ted. You need a vacation. You need to travel.

Ted If you've got nothing to do with that girl's disappearance, why didn't you contact us?

Elston I didn't know you were looking for me.

Ted It's been all over the news.

Elston I don't have a TV. Or a radio. I don't read newspapers.

Ted You know an awful lot of trivia for somebody who doesn't pay attention to the media.

Elston I said I don't read newspapers. I do pay attention. I do.

Ted Did you kill Sarah Casey?

Elston No. Did you? Is that why you're so unhappy?

Ted grabs Elston

Ted Listen you little sonofabitch: HELP ME.

Elston You don't want me to be guilty. I can tell.

Ted I don't give a good goddamn if you're guilty. GIVE ME SOME ANSWERS.

Elston You're kind, Ted. Like Sarah Casey. Why are you so unhappy?

Ted I HATE MY JOB I WISH I WAS ON THE TAKE MY WIFE'S ABOUT TO LEAVE ME I REALLY DON'T CARE AND I. CANNOT STAND. MY CHILDREN.

Ted releases Elston. A silence as Ted composes himself

Elston On that night. That Sunday night. I close the shop early. I don't know why. I decide to do inventory. I come across Timothy Creighton's tuxedo. Mrs Creighton had been in earlier that week. She always dry-cleans her donations. She's one of the few to observe that rule. And it is a rule, you see. Sometimes, I break the rule and accept unwashed clothing from customers I like. I don't know why. Mrs Creighton makes regular donations. I know her first name. She doesn't know mine. She never did. I wonder if that bothers her now. I've never met Mr Creighton. I find a business card in the left breast pocket of his tuxedo jacket. It's stained. Red wine, I think. I feel sorry for Mr Creighton. I don't know why. But in that

moment, I like him very much. I have to like a person to wear his clothes,
don't you? I put on the tux. I leave the shop. It is six-thirty. I go to Natalie's.
I drop off the week's receipts on Sunday nights. She hadn't felt well that
week. I had hoped she would allow me to take her to dinner. She wouldn't.
Allow me. I don't know why. I leave Natalie's. I head home. I get to the
front door and I find I can't insert my key into its lock. It occurs to me that
I should go to Timothy Creighton's house. But I don't. I don't know why.
I go to O'Malley's. I don't go to bars, but I go there. Men in bars laugh at
me. Because I'm so small. Because they're glad they're not that small.
Because I allow them to laugh. I am O'Malley's only customer that night.
I take an immediate liking to Jack Fallon. I begin to wish that he could be
my brother. And then. Sarah Casey enters the bar. I recognize her instantly
as the woman who had helped me plan a vacation two weeks earlier. You
didn't know that, did you, Ted? I went to her travel agency. I do that
frequently. Drop by. At different travel agencies. I talk to women who
work in travel agencies. It's the only time women are happy to speak to me.
When there's the possibility that I'll spend money in their business
establishments. I often offer to spend money on women I know. And they
never let me. I don't know why. Sarah Casey was the last travel agent I
spoke to. Of course, at the time, I was wearing the clothing of a Paul Jonas.
Poor Mr Jonas died on the QEII while he and his wife celebrated their
diamond jubilee. He never did get to wear his new suit. So. Wearing the
clothes of Paul Jonas, I, with the aid of Sarah Casey, plan a vacation I never
intend to take. I bought two packet trips, via Greyhound buses, to Atlantic
City. I left the travel agency and meant to rip up the tickets. But I didn't.
I don't know why. When I see Sarah at O'Malley's I feel it is fate. We talk.
Sarah confesses a desire to travel. I'm certain she doesn't recognize me. I
entertain her by proposing the possibility of differing scenarios. For her
life. Overall, I'm sure I present a very attractive portrait of Timothy J
Creighton. And while I like Sarah, I know she will not allow me to spend
money on her. She will not suggest a ride on the Circle Line. She will not.
Take a trip. With me. She tires. She wants to go home. I open the door for
her. She steps outside. I show her the bright, full moon. I point her in the
direction of the Holland Tunnel. There is a moment when our continuing
in the same direction is possible. She takes a step. I hesitate. It makes all
the difference. I watch her walk downtown. I watch her take steps. I stand
perfectly still. I call out to her. Sarah, I say, Sarah Casey: where are you
going? And then she disappears.

Ted (*after a silence*) Thank you.

Beat

Would you like ... a cup of coffee?

Elston Will you arrest me now?
Ted Would you prefer, I don't know, tea?
Elston Will I make you famous, Ted?
Ted Well. I'd rather you made me rich.
Elston I'm sorry about your wife. And your kids.
Ted Are you?
Elston Don't leave.
Ted I need some coffee.
Elston I like you, Ted. Why'd you let go of me? I liked it when you held me. I liked it.

SCENE 2

The same

Natalie and Timothy are waiting. It's clear each knows who the other is, but neither wants to commit to conversation

Timothy How could you hire somebody like that? There. I've said it. I had to say it.
Natalie I'm sure I don't understand what you're talking about.
Timothy I've never even met this man. Do you realize that? I'm here to identify a tuxedo.
Natalie He sells old clothing for me. That's all I know. And I don't think we're supposed to be chatting right now.
Timothy I'll probably lose my job over this.
Natalie Well ... I'm sorry.
Timothy No. You're not sorry. You're mortified. Mortified that you're involved in this at all.
Natalie But I'm not involved.

Beat

You're the lawyer, aren't you?
Timothy Yeah. Lucky me. Personally, I think you're the guiltiest party in this mess.
Natalie You're much more handsome than you appear to be on television. I've seen clips of your statement. You're actually very handsome.
Timothy Well. Thank you. (*Beat*) I've got to ask you this. I really do. Don't you screen applications for employment? Don't you ask for references?
Natalie This is the situation, Tim. May I call you that? May I call you Tim?
Timothy Timothy. I prefer Timothy. Actually.

Natalie Well then, Timothy. This is the situation. I inherit a ridiculous business from a dear but preposterous spinster aunt. I have no wish to sort through dirty old clothes. Now I ask you: is this an unreasonable position to take? It's a charity business. How is anybody supposed to make anything of it? Nevertheless, I respect my aunt's wishes and take over this — thrift place. And who do you think I can hire for the overwhelmingly tedious job of running the hovel on a daily basis? Would you do it, Timothy? No. I thought not. Furthermore, what do you suppose I can afford to pay the lucky recipient of this position? I can hardly be picky when we're talking a minimum wage type situation. Don't you agree? Yes, I thought you would. And so. How can you fault me for hiring a thoroughly agreeable — if somewhat odd — young man? He told me he was from Nebraska. He told me he was the child of farmers. He's polite. He's well-spoken. He's never stolen anything from me and he's not likely to leave his job and decide to become an artist. He took a polygraph. He passed. He's mine for life if I want him. What else should I have done? So he embellishes from time to time. He seems to have several wives and fiancées, all of whom he really can't keep straight from one conversation to the next, but ... who am I to judge? I think he's honest. And I believe he is telling the truth about the Casey girl's disappearance. He's always on time. He makes the customers laugh. And while it's true I would not choose to be his friend, I don't think that counts as proof of anything other than that he — he makes me nervous. In fact, he makes my skin crawl. He's not the kind of man I ordinarily talk to. He's small.

Timothy You hired a man who makes your skin crawl. You hired a man who wears other people's clothing.

Natalie Well. Coming from a thrift shop perspective, I don't find that at all unusual.

Timothy You don't.

Natalie Of course not. Look, he sells other people's clothing to other people all the time. Lots of people wear other people's clothing. I had no idea he was doing ... whatever he was doing ... and I thoroughly object to the practice but ——

Timothy You support him anyway.

Natalie I didn't say I support him.

Timothy You'll stick by him on this.

Natalie I didn't say that, either.

Timothy Most of the people I work with think I have something to do with this woman's disappearance.

Natalie Did you?

Timothy I said I didn't. The bartender said I didn't.

Natalie People lie. People are paid to lie.

Timothy You don't actually believe ——
Natalie I read it. In the *Post*. It's one theory.
Timothy Oh. I missed that one.
Natalie It's very interesting. You see, the theory is that you and the bartender are in it together.
Timothy I think I've heard a variation on this.
Natalie You take attractive young girls and sell them into the white slave trade. In California. Evidently, it's running rampant out there. And, the theory continues, you framed Elston. You know. Made it look like he did it. Or at least raised the serious possibility that he did it.
Timothy Did what?

Beat

Look. Is it just a coincidence he was wearing my suit? Or maybe — maybe the bartender and I hit him over the head, dressed him up in my suit, dragged him to the bar, sat him on a stool and waited until he woke up? And, naturally, he'd have no memory of such an event.
Natalie The *Post* didn't offer any details. It just made a couple of suppositions.
Timothy I could make a couple of suppositions about you.
Natalie No. You couldn't. My name is not being associated with, well, the more unsavoury aspects of this case.
Timothy Like you said. People accept money. To lie.
Natalie Meaning just what. Exactly.
Timothy Meaning. If I lose my job, I'd maybe take some money to say a few things about you.
Natalie Really, Tim, don't be ridiculous. You're being ridiculous.
Timothy People stare at me when I walk my dog.
Natalie I should be so lucky, Tim.
Timothy I'm angry. And CALL ME TIMOTHY, GODDAMNIT.
Natalie (*after a beat*) After this blows over, you can probably get a job anywhere. You'll be a celebrity. Who wouldn't want to hire somebody like you? The office gossip would be extraordinary. But what about me? All I'm left with is the same no-win business situation. What do you think I can do? Hang a sign outside: THIS IS THE PLACE WHERE IT MIGHT HAVE HAPPENED?
Timothy My privacy has been violated.
Natalie Whose hasn't? Sell your story. Beat them to the punch.
Timothy He was wearing my clothes. He might have killed a woman while he wore my tuxedo.
Natalie And she might have simply walked away. You know, this is not

exactly the Lindbergh case. Grown corpses really are hard to conceal. Not to mention there's been no evidence, none whatever, to connect Elston to anything other than having worn a tuxedo that didn't fit him.

Timothy People look at me and they see a criminal. And I cannot stop feeling guilty for something that somebody else did while I was holding my wife in my arms.

They sit in silence for a while

Natalie I just thought of something funny. You're here to identify a tuxedo. It's like identifying a body, except it's not. Isn't that funny?

Timothy Why are you here?

Natalie Oh. Well. Elston. He had nobody else to pick him up.

Timothy He's here? He's in this building now?

Natalie Yes. I think I'll do something nice for him this evening. Like take him to dinner. (*Beat*) Unless of course you'd rather come out to dinner with me. After you identify the tuxedo.

Timothy No. Thank you. I have ... reading. To catch up on.

Beat

Would you do me a favour? Would you ... tell me you don't believe I have anything to do with this? Because I'm beginning to doubt myself. Sometimes. Sometimes I think, well, what if. What if my wife hadn't cleaned out our closets that day. What if I had been home to stop her from giving away that tux. It didn't fit me anymore. But I liked it. You hold on to things that mean something to you.

Natalie I'm afraid I can't sympathize. I try not to wear anything more than once if I can help it.

Timothy Somebody's daughter is missing and possibly dead. And I can't escape the feeling that she, well, that she saw me that night. Or a part of me. I can't ... say anything else. About it.

Natalie OK. I don't believe you had anything to do with this.

Beat

Now. Why don't you come out with me for a drink? You really are a good-looking man. Much better looking than you appear to be. On television, I mean.

SCENE 3

Ellen's apartment

Ellen, Anthony and Ted. Ellen holds a half-crocheted blanket

Ted It's an empty room on the highway between Forty-Fourth and Forty-Fifth. Not a bed. Not a chair. Not one stick of furniture. Just ... globes. Of every conceivable size and shape. A globe of the moon. Of Mars. A geopolitical globe. A population density globe. And one file cabinet. Full of five-by-seven unlined white notepads. And on these notepads, neat rows of dates and times. No names. Just descriptions. Physical descriptions of people. Quite detailed. Like a diary which contains essentially the skeleton of information. The first entry reads: "Tall chestnut-haired man on southwest corner of Fifty-Seventh and Sixth. I thought he smiled at me. Was probably wiping a speck of dirt from the corner of his mouth". The last entry: "Pretty red-head, five-three, in elevator at Chrysler Building. I sneezed. She didn't notice". (*Beat*) I have never seen anything like his closet. An enormous walk-in inside which was all the furniture. An EZ chair. A captain's chair. A chipped maple bureau. An oak schoolboy's desk. An Army issue wool blanket. Three goose down pillows. And framed family photographs. Except on closer inspection, we discover they are the photographs that came with the frames. One frame still carries its price sticker. And there are very few articles of clothing. Almost none. (*Beat*) The bathroom is spotless. So is the kitchen. We find nothing. No hair. No fingerprints. Certainly, most certainly, we find no blood. In the medicine cabinet there's a four-year-old empty prescription bottle of Tylenol with codeine. On the fridge is taped a postcard of Napoleon's tomb. Postmarked at the GPO on Thirty-Third and Eight. It's addressed to Elston and carries no message. Inside the fridge, one mouldy grapefruit. One unopened box of Devil Dogs. An eight-ounce can of Campbell's V-Eight juice. An airline-sized bottle of Stolichynaya vodka. (*Beat*) The only eating utensils are plastic. Four knives, two forks, seven spoons, neatly stacked in a plastic cutlery tray. Two plastic dinner plates. One ceramic coffee mug. One soup bowl, badly chipped. A broken two-slice toaster. A roulette wheel ashtray from Resorts International, Atlantic City. A Manhattan residential telephone directory in which are circled in red felt pen the numbers of well-known people. He has no telephone, but he was written a listing for himself in the directory. He wrote it in black ink.

An uncomfortable silence

Ellen So, Officer, this is very interesting and all, but I don't see why you gotta tell us the contents of this creep's refrigerator. My baby girl is dead and you're telling me about tomato juice?

Ted In going over the details, there is the possibility of finding clues.

Anthony Where's this guy now? He's out on the street? You let him go?

Ted He's co-operated. He asked us to examine his apartment. He's told us his version of events, which does not differ significantly from Jack Fallon's version of events. Except, of course, that Elston Rupp does not recall Jack Fallon's self-confessed heroics.

Anthony So this guy, this little fuck, he's out and walking around?

Ted Would you like me to arrest him for impersonating an entertainment attorney?

Ellen HE MURDERED MY DAUGHTER. DROWNED HER IN A BATHTUB.

Ted We have nothing to substantiate that.

Ellen Yeah, well, you got nothing that doesn't prove it, do you?

Ted I don't know what to tell you.

Anthony You believe this guy?

Ted I am tending toward it, yes.

Ellen You believe this faggot psycho who walks around in dirty clothes but you don't believe normal people like us?

Ted You weren't there. He was. Listen to me. I would bet that if you rounded up, at random, two or three dozen guys who live in a ten-block radius, you'd find that they'd all tell more or less the same sad story. The exact same story of their lives, Mrs Casey. The details would not significantly differ from man to man.

Anthony I got a friend, this guy I grew up with in Bay Ridge? Since he was a kid, he's been collecting his girlfriend's toenail clippings. Can you imagine? Puts them in a shoe box.

Ellen Whatsa matter with you, Anthony? You taking his side? You taking the side of a pervert?

Anthony Mrs Casey, no offence. You know, it's just — some guys, they're weird.

Ted Yes. Some guys are weird.

Ellen I'm sitting here with a couple of professional fucking Freuds and neither of them can tell me what's happened to my daughter.

Ted Perhaps she did simply leave. Go away. Escape.

Ellen My daughter would never ESCAPE. She wasn't the type. Besides, she was gonna get married. She was gonna go to Sicily on her honeymoon. We was all gonna go. Personally, I wasn't big on the idea of Italy. But at my age, I'd take anything. Right, Anthony?

Anthony Mrs Casey, she didn't wanna marry me. I mean, we gotta give her some due. The girl said she did not want to marry me.

Ted Is that true, Mrs Casey?
Ellen What does he know? What? He cuts hair for a living. That's not normal. My daughter, she — oh what's the point. I don't care. I don't. Whether she's dead or gone to New Jersey or if she's camped out on the ROOF. I DON'T CARE.

Another uncomfortable silence

Ted There won't be an arrest. I'm sorry. I think that Sarah is alive. I hope ... you get a phone call or a note that says, "Hi mom. I've decided to become a Shaker and I'm making furniture in Pennsylvania." (*Beat*) I have nothing else to offer at the moment.
Ellen Hey, hey — WAIT. You can't go. Where's my satisfaction? Huh? WHAT AM I LEFT WITH?
Ted I don't know. Another blanket?

Ted exits

Ellen holds up the unfinished blanket

Ellen I called my daughter a booze bag. That's the last thing I said to her.

Ellen cries. Anthony tries to dry her tears away with the blanket

Scene 4

The police station

Elston and Natalie

Elston Thank you for coming. Are you mad at me?
Natalie Why would I be mad at you?
Elston A day's revenue. Lost.
Natalie Well. You'll make it up to me.
Elston How?

Beat

Natalie Elston. Is everything, well, is it all OK now? Did you — fix it?
Elston I'm not arrested. If that's what you mean.
Natalie Good. I'm glad it's over.
Elston It's not over. There's the girl.

Natalie Of course. The girl.

Beat

We can't help that, Elston. We don't know where she is.
Elston Yes, we do.
Natalie We do?
Elston Yes. She's elsewhere. (*Beat*) Are you going to fire me?
Natalie Probably not.
Elston Are you going to give me a raise?
Natalie No. Well. Eventually.
Elston That's OK. I don't need money.
Natalie Elston, everybody needs money.
Elston I used to think so.

Beat

I had some people over at my apartment this morning.
Natalie I wasn't aware you had any friends.
Elston I don't. They were detectives. Men with magnifying glasses.
Natalie Oh. That must have been exciting. Or something.
Elston I invited them. But I shouldn't have.
Natalie I imagine they would have invited themselves into your apartment
if you hadn't extended the courtesy.
Elston That's an odd concept. Extending courtesy. Like extending a hand.

Beat

Do you know where I live?
Natalie Uhm. No. Yes, yes — I mean, I read about it. In the *Post*. But your
address wasn't given out. Not exactly.
Elston Too bad.
Natalie Why would you want a bunch of strangers knowing your address?
Elston You're not a stranger.

Beat

I live on the highway. Well. Above the highway. In a room. I can see the
traffic.
Natalie That's ... pleasant.
Elston I watch the traffic and think, where are you all going? Why don't you
stop a while? Slow down. And then I realize I shouldn't be concerned about

speeding cars when I don't even know who my neighbours are. Or if I even
have any neighbours. My building might very well be deserted. Except for
me.

Natalie People make noise. They cook. You'd know if they were there.

Elston I don't cook.

Natalie Well. Neither do I. So. There you go.

Elston Let me take you to dinner.

Natalie No. I can't. I have ... a friend. From out of town. Visiting.

Elston Oh. A traveller.

Natalie Why don't you see a movie?

Elston I don't see movies.

Natalie Oh, come on. An insignificant little comedy, something to take your
    mind off ——

Elston Nothing is insignificant. (*Beat*) What an interesting phrase: take
    one's mind off. Have you ever noticed how most of the language we use
    to suggest mental activity conjures up a violent physical action? Take one's
    mind off. Off his rocker.

Beat

I have to go home now. I have to watch traffic.

Natalie Elston, I've got to ask you a really big favour. I know you've got a
    load on your — what I mean is. Well, would you please not wear the
    customers' clothes anymore? I don't want to be a bitch, but. It's probably
    unsanitary.

Elston Give and take.

Natalie If it was up to me, I would let you borrow ... whatever ... you know.

Elston It is up to you.

Natalie The customers are horrified.

Elston How do you know? You're never there.

Beat

The favour. What's the favour you want?

Natalie That. I just asked you. About the clothes.

Elston Don't you want me to buy you groceries? Or flowers?

Natalie I hate flowers. And I don't cook. Remember?

Elston I might move to New Jersey.

Natalie Why would you do that? It's across the river.

Elston Well. You won't allow me to offer you any courtesy. But I can offer
    you my hand. (*He extends his hand*)

Natalie Elston. This is a little weird, isn't it?

Elston We're friends.

Natalie We ... know each other. A bit. Yes.
Elston Shake my hand. Please.
Natalie (*after a pause*) I'll see you tomorrow. At the shop. Don't be
ridiculous.

Elston drops his hand

Elston You've been very kind. I think. I — I'll open the shop early
tomorrow. I'll make it up to you. I think. I think — good-night. Natalie.
Natalie Yes. Um. *Ciao.*

Elston exits

Natalie lights a cigarette. She doesn't smoke it

Ted enters

Natalie I meant to be nice to him. Take him to dinner. Buy him a drink.
Something. But I couldn't. He. He makes my skin crawl.

SCENE 5

O'Malley's saloon

Jack is at the bar. Timothy stands, looking around

Timothy I had to see it. For myself. I hope you don't mind.
Jack No skin off my back, bud.
Timothy It's hard to believe, but I've never been this far west.
Jack Yeah? Do you like it?
Timothy I've lived in New York eighteen years and I've never seen this part
of town. I imagined, I don't know, something different.
Jack Yeah. I know. People think all sorts of things. Tough things.
Timothy Show me where she sat.
Jack Huh?
Timothy Sarah Casey. That night. Where did she sit?
Jack (*indicating the barstool*) It ain't a shrine, mister.
Timothy (*sitting on the barstool*) Did she sit like this?
Jack Yeah. I guess. To tell you the truth, it's kinda fuzzy to me now.
Timothy And Rupp. Where did he sit?
Jack Someplace else. I don't know. Funny how your memory goes, real
quick like.
Timothy They walked out that door together. And Sarah Casey was never

seen again. Rupp touched that doorknob. The night appeared. And she was gone.

Beat

I dream about this.

Jack Lemme give you some advice, pal. Forget it. You wasn't even here. Me, now I was here. And I can't even remember where the fuck they sat. It's better that way.

Timothy Better for whom?

Jack You got to grab your bull by its horns. Like me. Take me, right? I'm buying a new sign, some of that fancy neon. I call the bar *Sarah Casey's* now. Didya know that?

Timothy Well. Congratulations.

Jack I figure, Sarah, she was a tough kid. She woulda appreciated my business sense. She's gone, it don't matter. She comes back, she'll be honoured to have the place named after her.

Timothy A beacon on the highway.

Jack Huh?

Timothy A candle in the window.

Jack Yeah, sure. Candles in windows. That's good. I might do that. Like I said, you gotta figure your angle on every situation. What's your angle on this, mister?

Timothy I'm in therapy.

Jack Whoa, buddy. Heavy shit.

Timothy Don't you think your life has been altered in some way? I mean, I might be having dinner with my kids now. But I'm not. You might be shooting the shit with Sarah Casey now. If not for this.

Jack Nope. I think ... we're doing exactly what we're meant to be doing. And I think there's reasons for what we're doing but fuck me if I know what they are.

Timothy Has business picked up since — since the, uh, name change?

Jack Nah. But it could. I betcha it could.

Timothy Elston Rupp. That's one of those names. A name from another universe.

Jack Yeah. A real ... farmer name.

Timothy (*after a pause*) I'd like a drink.

Jack Sure. Listen, it's on me. What'll you have?

Timothy Stoly Martini. Olives.

Beat

Did you really make Rupp for a killer when he walked through that door?

Jack Personally, between me and you — this is between me and you, right?

Timothy Right.

Jack Look, I couldn't tell a killer from a fucking priest. But Rupp's not talking and she's not here, right?

Timothy Right.

Jack But I did win the Golden Gloves. I swear.

SCENE 6

The thrift shop

Elston is behind the counter. Ted carries a box of clothing

Ted I've brought some things.

Elston Are they clean?

Ted I washed them myself. Ironed everything. Even the socks.

Elston Why?

Ted Why not?

Elston I mean, why here? Don't you have a local thrift shop?

Ted I want to keep in touch.

Elston You feel you know me.

Ted I don't know you.

Elston You've dusted my apartment for fingerprints. You feel you're entitled.

Ted Look. I'm just donating some clothes. I'm sorry.

Elston I'm sorry for you. Are you sorry for me?

Ted I'm troubled by you.

Elston I burned my notepads. You read them.

Ted I browsed through them.

Elston Why didn't you read them?

Ted It wasn't necessary.

Elston It was necessary. If you wanted to know me. But you don't. So.

Ted There are unresolved questions. I'd like to ask you. But.

Elston I won't answer your questions anymore, Ted. Because if I answered them, you wouldn't come back here.

Ted If you answer me, I won't bother you again.

Elston Bother me, Ted.

Beat

I hope Sarah Casey's in Winchester.

Ted So do I.

Elston People from all over the city come in here just to look at me. Do you think they're afraid of me?

Ted Do they look you in the eye?

Elston Never. I had this thought yesterday: before Sarah Casey disappeared, I probably stood a better chance of making eye contact with a person, even though I was anonymous. Now. Well, I couldn't tell you the eye colour of anybody who's been here in the last week. (*Beat*) You don't look me in the eye, Ted.

Ted Maybe you should get another job.

Elston Do you think I could be a detective?

Ted Well, if you can't stand people fearing you, then police work is not ideal.

Elston I didn't say I couldn't stand it. You can't stand it, though.

Beat

I don't see Natalie anymore. She has a messenger pick up the week's receipts on Sunday nights. The messenger brings me my paycheque. There's a different messenger each week. So there's some variety. I see more people that way.

Ted You watched that woman walk away. Tell me you watched her walk away.

Elston Last week, the messenger asked me for my autograph. It was thrilling. But he thought I was the lawyer. He thought I was Timothy Creighton.

Ted Verify it for me. Please.

Elston There's some irony in this, Ted.

Ted People just don't disappear.

Elston I know that.

Beat

You'll need a receipt. For the clothes.

Ted Maybe you're right. I should bring them someplace closer to home.

Elston I knew you weren't the type to give away your old clothes. You hoard things. People. Faces. You can't stand the thought of other people in your pants.

Ted I'll go now.

Elston I thrive on all things second-hand.

Ted Well. I guess that's why you like me.

Beat

Goodbye, Elston.

Elston You'll come back.

Ted Anything's possible.
Elston You're mine.

Ted exits

Elston begins to undress

I can't wear clothes at all anymore. I'm doing this favour for Natalie.

SCENE 7

O'Malley's saloon

Elston, Sarah and Jack, as they were in Scene One. Music: "Happy Together" by The Turtles

Elston The fascinating thing about being an entertainment attorney is that you meet people who have problems you couldn't begin to imagine. It makes one feel better about one's own problems.
Sarah I don't guess you have many problems. You have money.
Elston I carry the burden of all my clients' sadness.
Sarah That is such bullshit. You hear this guy, Jack? He's talking about carrying burdens.
Jack Burdens are what animals carry.
Elston I'm an animal. Aren't you an animal, Jack?
Jack Hey, I like animals. But I ain't no animal.
Elston It would be simpler. To be an animal.
Jack You couldn't protect yourself. You'd be at the mercy of other animals. Bigger animals.
Elston What if you had teeth? And say you were seven feet tall. You couldn't think, certainly. But you could protect yourself. Seeking protection is a primary animal instinct.
Sarah I wanna be a fish. Then I could swim. A lot.
Elston You could swim away. The earth, Sarah Casey, is seventy-five per cent water. And so are we.
Sarah Yeah, but I'd wanna be a slim fish. A pretty fish. And that way, I wouldn't last long. I'd get eaten up in a hurry. Or else end up in some sadistic kid's fish tank.
Elston Why does the kid have to be sadistic?
Sarah Well. Let's just say it's my burden.
Jack I hadda mute parrot when I was a kid. Christ. I wish I had tortured it.
Sarah Oh, man. I really wanna get out of here.
Elston People always say "I wanna get out". And they rarely mean it. They rarely walk away. We stay. We don't take steps.

Sarah That's easy for you to say, Mister-Entertainment-Attorney-to-the-Stars.

Elston What if I told you that I live in one room. That I use no furniture. That I sleep in a closet. Would you believe me?

Sarah Whaddya think, Jack? You believe this guy sleeps in a closet?

Jack No way. This guy, he sleeps on a fucking king-sized waterbed.

Sarah Yeah. And he's got some obnoxious bitch wife who spends all his money. And he loves it.

Elston I like the bit about the money. Go on.

Jack He's got a Swiss bank account. And he ... collects. Yeah, he collects like, mink stoles. Sells them to the Japs.

Elston Ermine. It would have to be Ermine.

Sarah He's got a castle in Germany. On the Rhine. That's a river, Jack. And he wants to teach his wife how to waltz, but she's too pigheaded to learn. It frustrates him. A lot.

Elston That's perfect. So far.

Sarah So. He likes to dance and he would love to learn Greek, but his fucking mother is always criticizing him about it. Constant ridicule. He doesn't have any close friends. And he's trapped in this loveless marriage he doesn't have a clue how to get out of.

Elston And what does he do about this?

Sarah He ... doesn't know. He feels like a fake, like he's not entitled to something different because he doesn't have any money.

Elston But he has a castle on the Rhine.

Sarah Right. But it's ... it's his mother's castle. She's evil and she won't give him NOTHING. And he he he — lives in one room with a a a single bed and a desk with nothing in it and her only hope the only piece of comfort she has is a stupid old record nailed to her stupid old wall which is painted pink cause her bitch of a mother says pink is for GIRLS and she clings to this delusion that the record was written for her and she thinks that means she's entitled to go SOMEWHERE SHE'S NEVER BEEN. (*Beat*) Which, for her, is just about everywhere. She knows the name of practically every shit hole in this wide wide world but she's only seen the names on maps. She'll probably marry a good-natured man who she won't love, because at least then she can take a vacation. But basically, she thinks she'll drink until she drops.

Elston And then?

Sarah Something endless and black. She'll have a kid 'cause she's got nothing better to do. She'll be tempted to drown the kid, but she won't. Because she is not an animal, even though maybe she would like to be a fish. But she can't swim. 'Cause she never learned.

Elston And then, having no other option, she will walk on air.

Sarah He's talking shit again, Jack. Just when I was beginning to like him a little.

Elston I'm talking about miracles, Sarah. Our capacity to accept the impossible increases exponentially when we are at the ends of our ropes.

Beat

Are you really beginning to like me?

Sarah I got a soft spot for religious fanatics.

Elston Have you ever been at the end of your rope, Sarah?

Sarah Sure. Can't you see my rope burns?

Elston I have them, too.

Sarah Yeah. Well. We can march in a parade some day and reminisce about our war wounds.

Elston I can walk on air.

Sarah God. I wish that was true. I do.

Elston If I could walk on air, it would be the most strange and wondrous sight, no?

Jack The strangest thing I ever seen was my mother burying this mouse she killed in a trap. She breaks the thing's neck, right? And then she goes all soft and wants to bury it in the fucking backyard. And get this, like, she wants to dress it up in something nice. And the only nice thing she's got is my christening robe. I say, Ma, whaddya wacko or something? And she says, Jack, it'd be a sin not to bury this mouse in a soft white robe and since you're just too dumb to have kids, I don't expect you'll be needing it. (*Beat*) And I had to agree with her.

Sarah Thank you, Jack. You've proved once and for all that it's possible for men to walk on air. Thank you.

Elston What's the strangest thing you've ever seen, Sarah?

Sarah Well. Aside from the sight of me in my mother's house? Let's see. I'd have to say ... this guy. He comes into the travel shop a couple of week ago. He's got this map in his pocket. The map's so old and so worn it looks like it's come outta the womb with this guy. He asks me to close my eyes and pick a vacation destination for him off this map. But it's a map of the tri-state metropolitan area. He insists I choose. And so. I close my eyes and I pick the Holland Tunnel. This guy is so ... so grateful. His desire to go anywhere — just to go — is so strong. So well defined. He has such trust. In me. And suddenly I feel the desire to kiss him, full on the lips, for a very long time. Because really, he has as little idea of where to go or what to do as I have. I don't kiss him. I don't take him by his hand and lead him into the world. I am eyeball to eyeball with a man who's the only person I'm likely to meet who fully understands the desire to simply ... vanish. And I send him into a tunnel.

Elston That's the saddest story I've ever heard.

Sarah I know. Don't you think I know that?

Elston Maybe you'll meet that man again. And you'll walk on air. Together.

Sarah I wouldn't know him if he bit me in the ass.

Elston You can make the choice to remember. I do. You can take steps. What do you think, Jack? Can you take steps?

Jack Yeah, sure. I step outta my apartment, I step outta my car, I step in my bar, I step back out to my car, I step back into my apartment. Lotta steps, I'm taking.

Sarah Look. It's been nice, guys. But. Time to face the music. Time for beddie-bye. Time to imagine myself falling asleep to something other than the sounds of hookers getting pissed on the highway.

Elston The waves lapping gently past your castle on the Rhine.

Sarah Sure. Fairy-tales do come true it can happen to you. If you're deluded at heart.

Beat

I'm so ... something ... I can't even push myself to walk. I gotta stop drinking and start walking.

Elston Let me help you to the door. I have a long walk ahead of me. It's time I started off.

Jack That's a fuck of a long walk, mister, to the East Side.

Elston Not if you walk on air.

Sarah Whaddya think, Jack? Am I stepping out with a lawyer or with some maniac who drowns women in his bathtub?

Jack shrugs

Elston (*opening the door*) Does it matter, Sarah Casey?

A beat, as she considers this

Sarah Makes no difference to me. But I sure hope you do walk on air. 'Cause it would be something to see.

Elston Our potential to walk on air is infinite. Shall we?

Elston bows to Sarah with a flourish as he holds the door open for her

Sarah exits

A beat, then Elston follows her out, the door remaining open behind him

Black-out

FURNITURE AND PROPERTY LIST

Only essential furniture and properties are listed here, as mentioned in the text. Further dressing may be added at the director's discretion

ACT I

SCENE 1

On stage: Bar. *On it and under it:* beer, glasses, spirits, mixers, olives, etc.

Personal: **Sarah**: cigarettes, matches

SCENE 2

On stage: Nil

SCENE 3

On stage: Nil

SCENE 4

On stage: Counter

Personal: **Elston**: glasses, moustache, map of New York metropolitan area

SCENE 5

On stage: Nil

Personal: **Elston**: box of "Fannie Farmer" chocolates, large envelope containing receipts, box of matches

SCENE 6

On stage: Microphones

Personal: **Ellen**: baby photos, 45rpm record

SCENE 7

On stage: Microphones
                Tabloid (**Ellen**)

SCENE 8

On stage: Counter
                Full-length mirror
                Clothes

ACT II

SCENE 1

On stage: Nil

SCENE 2

On stage: Nil

SCENE 3

On stage: Nil

Personal: **Ellen**: half-crocheted blanket

SCENE 4

On stage: Nil

Personal: **Natalie**: cigarettes, lighter

SCENE 5

On stage: Bar, drinks, glasses, etc.

SCENE 6

On stage: Counter

Personal: **Ted**: box containing clothing

SCENE 7

On stage: Bar, drinks, glasses, etc.

LIGHTING PLOT

Practical fittings required: nil

Various interior scenes

ACT I, SCENE 1

To open: Dim House Lights; bring up general lighting

Cue 1   **Elston**: "I shall. Sit a while. Sit."   (Page 10)
               Crossfade to press conference

ACT I, SCENE 2

Cue 2   **Jack**: "I won. Twice."   (Page 11)
               *Crossfade to **Ellen**'s apartment*

ACT I, SCENE 3

Cue 3   **Ellen**: " ... ice-cream now, huh?"   (Page 12)
               Crossfade to travel agency

ACT I, SCENE 4

Cue 4   **Elston**: "And not in coincidence. Don't you?"   (Page 17)
               *Crossfade to **Natalie**'s apartment*

ACT I, SCENE 5

Cue 5   **Elston**: "Why'd you do that?"   (Page 21)
               Crossfade to press conference

ACT I, SCENE 6

Cue 6   **Ellen**: "When she comes home."   (Page 23)
               *Crossfade to **Ellen**'s apartment*

ACT I, SCENE 7

Cue 7   **Sarah**: "Don't wait up."   (Page 27)
               Crossfade to thrift shop

Disappeared   55

ACT I, S<small>CENE</small> 8

Cue 8   **Elston** holds out his hands   (Page 28)
             Black-out

ACT II, S<small>CENE</small> 1

To open: Full stage lighting

Cue 9   **Elston**: "I liked it."   (Page 35)
             Crossfade to another part of the police station

ACT II, S<small>CENE</small> 2

Cue 10   **Natalie**: "On television, I mean."   (Page 38)
             *Crossfade to **Ellen**'s apartment*

ACT II, S<small>CENE</small> 3

Cue 11   **Anthony** tries to dry **Ellen**'s tears away   (Page 41)
             Crossfade to police station

ACT II, S<small>CENE</small> 4

Cue 12   **Natalie**: "He makes may skin crawl."   (Page 44)
             Crossfade to O'Malley's saloon

ACT II, S<small>CENE</small> 5

Cue 13   **Jack**: "I swear."   (Page 46)
             Crossfade to thrift shop

ACT II, S<small>CENE</small> 6

Cue 14   **Elston**: " ... this favour for Natalie."   (Page 48)
             Crossfade to O'Malley's saloon

ACT II, S<small>CENE</small> 7

Cue 15   **Elston** follows **Sarah** out   (Page 51)
             Black-out

EFFECTS PLOT

ACT I

Cue 1   As the House Lights dim   (Page 1)
         Music: "Eleanor" by The Turtles; fade a few minutes
             into the scene

Cue 2   **Elston**: " ... money on you."   (Page 19)
         The telephone rings four times

Cue 3   At opening   (Page 23)
         Music: "Paper Doll" by the Mills Brothers; fade when ready

ACT II

Cue 4   To open SCENE 7   (Page 48)
         Music: "Happy Together" by The Turtles; fade when ready